Cross Stitch

Seasonal Samplers

Celebrate the seasons with these charming sampler designs.

Designs by Alma Lynne Hayden

LEISURE ARTS, INC. • Maumelle, Arkansas

The Birds and the Bees

Celebrate spring and summer with these delightful designs!

The Soft Summer Breeze

The Birds and the Bees
Stitch Count = 108w × 124h

FABRIC SIZE

- One 15" × 17" (38.1cm × 43.2cm) piece of 14-ct. white aida

DESIGN SIZE

- 11-ct. = 9⅞" × 11¼" (25.1cm × 28.6cm)
- 14-ct. = 7¾" × 8⅞" (19.7cm × 22.5cm)
- 16-ct. = 6¾" × 7¾" (17.1cm × 19.7cm)

CROSS STITCH

ANCHOR		DMC	COLOR
002	•	White	White
400	B	317	Pewter Gray
9046	R	321	Christmas Red
265	U	471	Very Light Avocado Green
253	D	472	Ultra Light Avocado Green
168	K	597	Turquoise
167	C	598	Light Turquoise
295	Z	726	Light Topaz
302	J	743	Medium Yellow
301	F	744	Pale Yellow
158	E	747	Very Light Sky Blue
1012	P	754	Light Peach
1021	Y	761	Light Salmon
1004	M	920	Medium Copper
1003	G	921	Copper
1033	6	932	Light Antique Blue
1011	L	948	Very Light Peach
382	V	3371	Black Brown
035	N	3705	Dark Melon
1032	2	3752	Very Light Antique Blue
1031	H	3753	Ultra Very Light Antique Blue
1037	T	3756	Ultra Very Light Baby Blue
122	S	3807	Cornflower Blue
928	3	3811	Very Light Turquoise

FRENCH KNOT

ANCHOR		DMC	COLOR
382	•	3371	Black Brown

BACKSTITCH

ANCHOR		DMC	COLOR
1006	(green line)	304	Medium Christmas Red
295	(yellow line)	726	Light Topaz
261	(blue line)	3053	Green Gray
382	(black line)	3371	Black Brown
373	(orange line)	3828	Hazelnut Brown

The Birds and the Bees A

The Birds and the Bees B

The Birds and the Bees C

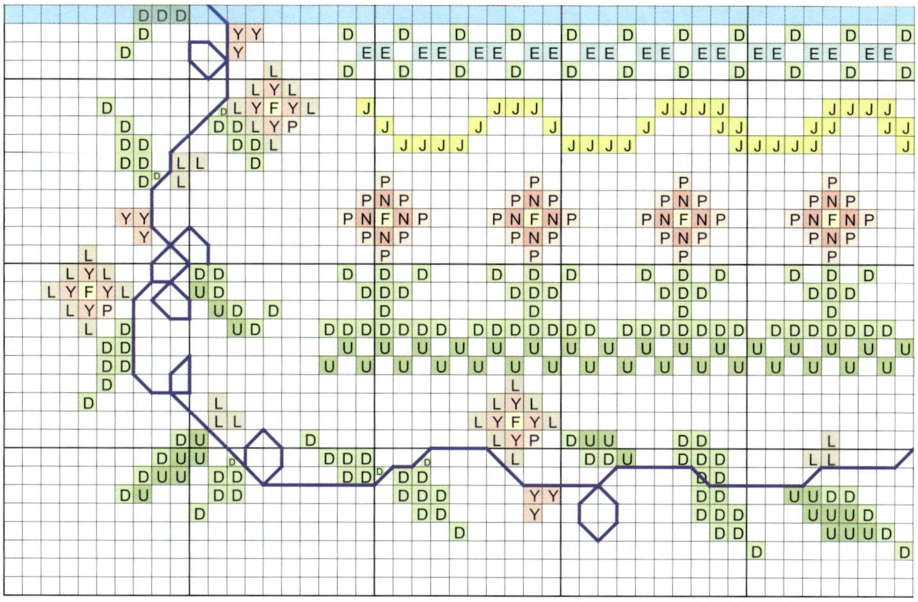

The Birds and the Bees Chart Diagram

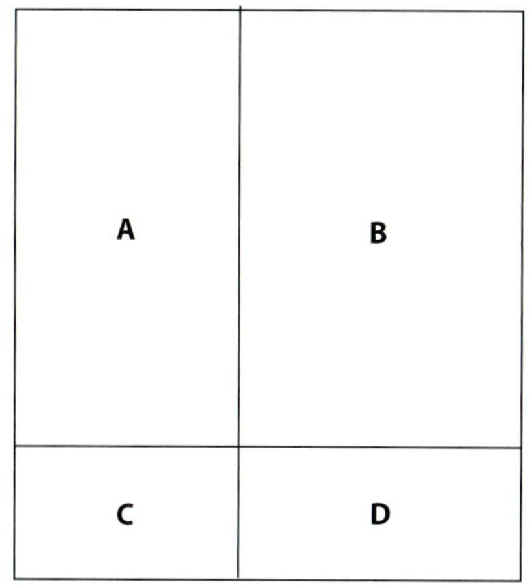

The Birds and the Bees D

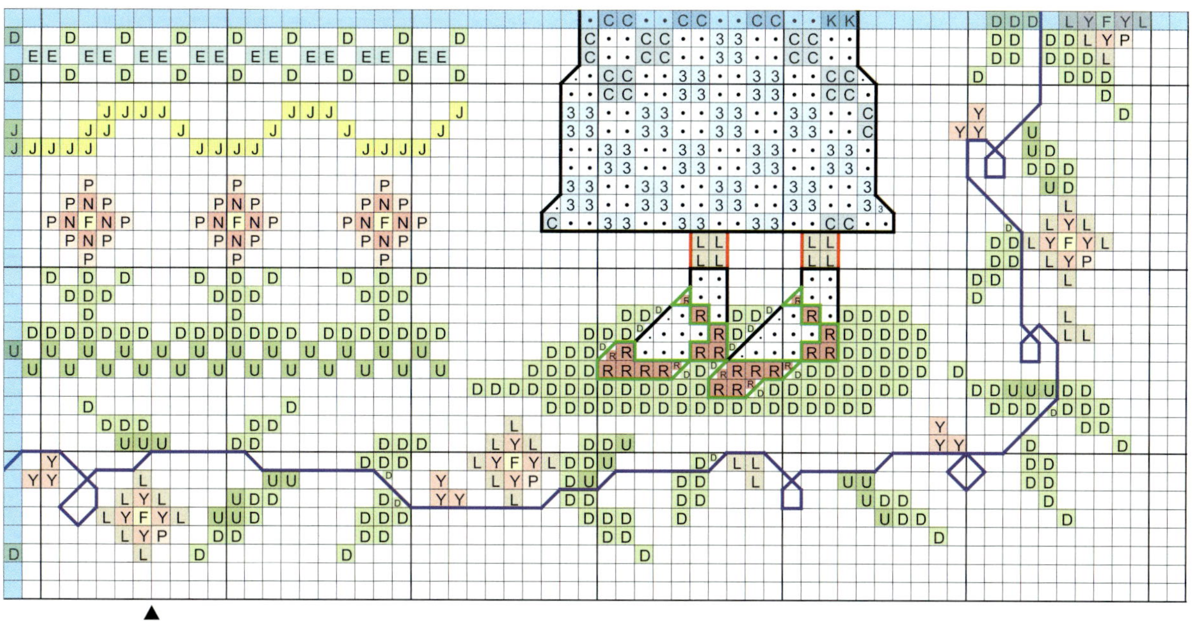

CROSS STITCH

ANCHOR		DMC	COLOR
002	•	White	White
400	B	317	Pewter Gray
9046	R	321	Christmas Red
265	U	471	Very Light Avocado Green
253	D	472	Ultra Light Avocado Green
168	K	597	Turquoise
167	C	598	Light Turquoise
295	Z	726	Light Topaz
302	J	743	Medium Yellow
301	F	744	Pale Yellow
158	E	747	Very Light Sky Blue
1012	P	754	Light Peach

CROSS STITCH

ANCHOR		DMC	COLOR
1021	Y	761	Light Salmon
1004	M	920	Medium Copper
1003	G	921	Copper
1033	6	932	Light Antique Blue
1011	L	948	Very Light Peach
382	V	3371	Black Brown
035	N	3705	Dark Melon
1032	2	3752	Very Light Antique Blue
1031	H	3753	Ultra Very Light Antique Blue
1037	T	3756	Ultra Very Light Baby Blue
122	S	3807	Cornflower Blue
928	3	3811	Very Light Turquoise

FRENCH KNOT

ANCHOR		DMC	COLOR
382	•	3371	Black Brown

BACKSTITCH

ANCHOR		DMC	COLOR
1006	green line	304	Medium Christmas Red
295	yellow line	726	Light Topaz
261	blue line	3053	Green Gray
382	black line	3371	Black Brown
373	orange line	3828	Hazelnut Brown

Bright blue area indicates last row of previous section of design.

The Soft Summer Breeze A

The Soft Summer Breeze B

The Soft Summer Breeze
Stitch Count = 106w × 124h

FABRIC SIZE

- One 15" × 17" (38.1cm × 43.2cm) piece of 14-ct. white aida

DESIGN SIZE

- 11-ct. = 9 5/8" × 11 1/4" (24.4cm × 28.6cm)
- 14-ct. = 7 1/2" × 8 7/8" (19.1cm × 22.5cm)
- 16-ct. = 6 5/8" × 7 3/4" (16.8cm × 19.7cm)

CROSS STITCH

ANCHOR		DMC	COLOR
002	•	White	White
1006	J	304	Medium Christmas Red
9046	6	321	Christmas Red
253	M	472	Ultra Light Avocado Green
168	G	597	Turquoise
167	R	598	Light Turquoise
238	B	703	Chartreuse
256	S	704	Bright Chartreuse
295	I	726	Light Topaz
293	N	727	Very Light Topaz
302	9	743	Medium Yellow
301	d	744	Pale Yellow
158	Q	747	Very Light Sky Blue
1012	a	754	Light Peach
1022	t	760	Salmon
1021	7	761	Light Salmon
1011	O	948	Very Light Peach
035	K	3705	Dark Melon
1037	T	3756	Ultra Very Light Baby Blue
122	H	3807	Cornflower Blue
928	W	3811	Very Light Turquoise

FRENCH KNOT

ANCHOR		DMC	COLOR
351	•	400	Dark Mahogany

BACKSTITCH

ANCHOR		DMC	COLOR
1006	—	304	Medium Christmas Red
400	—	317	Pewter Gray
351	—	400	Dark Mahogany
900	—	648	Light Beaver Gray
226	—	702	Kelly Green
295	—	726	Light Topaz
382	—	3371	Black Brown
373	—	3828	Hazelnut Brown

Bright blue area indicates last row of previous section of design.

The Soft Summer Breeze C

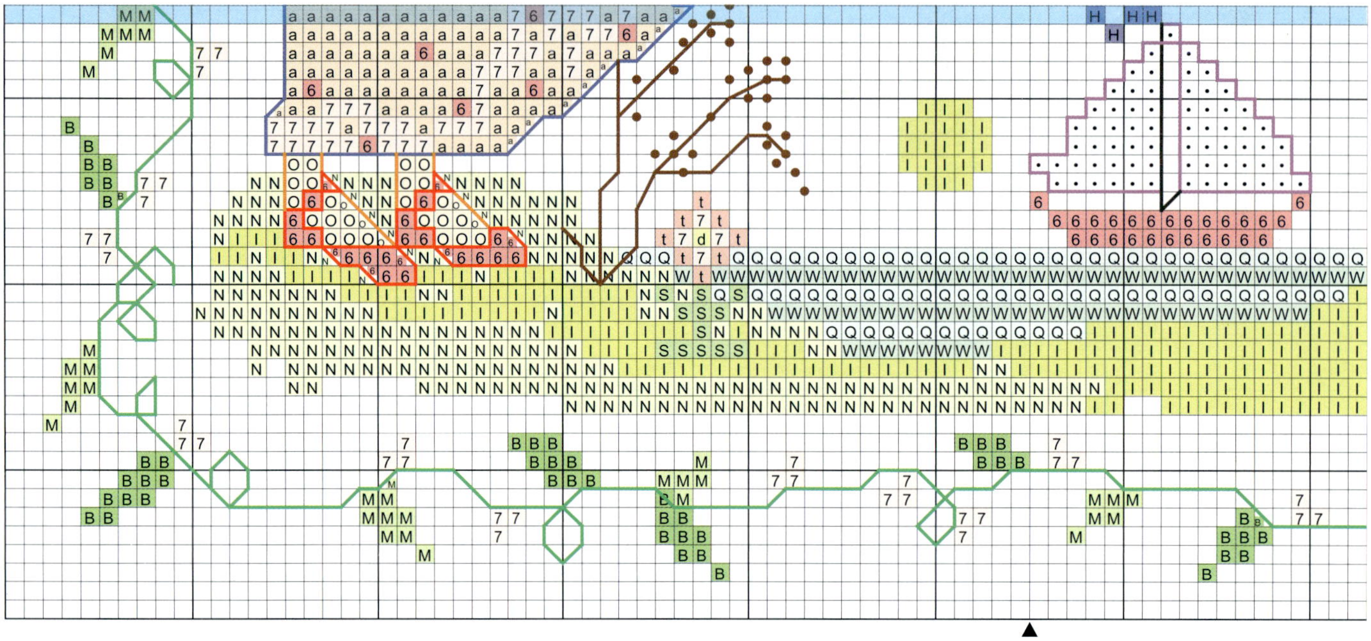

The Soft Summer Breeze D

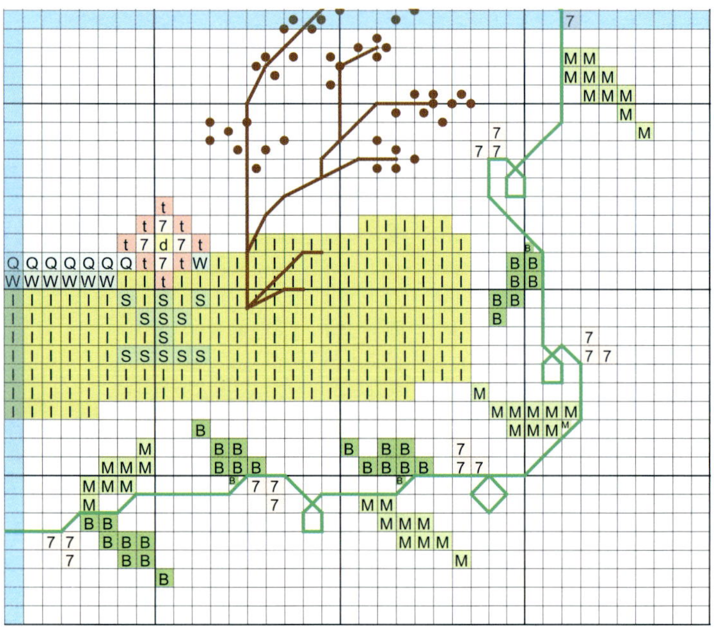

The Soft Summer Breeze Chart Diagram

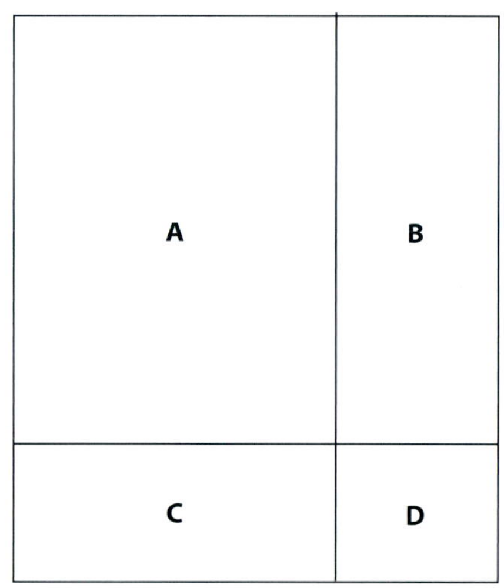

CROSS STITCH

ANCHOR		DMC	COLOR
002	•	White	White
1006	J	304	Medium Christmas Red
9046	6	321	Christmas Red
253	M	472	Ultra Light Avocado Green
168	G	597	Turquoise
167	R	598	Light Turquoise
238	B	703	Chartreuse
256	S	704	Bright Chartreuse
295	I	726	Light Topaz
293	N	727	Very Light Topaz
302	9	743	Medium Yellow
301	d	744	Pale Yellow

CROSS STITCH

ANCHOR		DMC	COLOR
158	Q	747	Very Light Sky Blue
1012	a	754	Light Peach
1022	t	760	Salmon
1021	7	761	Light Salmon
1011	O	948	Very Light Peach
035	K	3705	Dark Melon
1037	T	3756	Ultra Very Light Baby Blue
122	H	3807	Cornflower Blue
928	W	3811	Very Light Turquoise

FRENCH KNOT

ANCHOR		DMC	COLOR
351	•	400	Dark Mahogany

BACKSTITCH

ANCHOR		DMC	COLOR
1006	—	304	Medium Christmas Red
400	—	317	Pewter Gray
351	—	400	Dark Mahogany
900	—	648	Light Beaver Gray
226	—	702	Kelly Green
295	—	726	Light Topaz
382	—	3371	Black Brown
373	—	3828	Hazelnut Brown

Bright blue area indicates last row of previous section of design.

The Falling Leaves

Enjoy the beauty of fall and wintry delights with these lovely samplers.

The Snowcapped Trees

The Falling Leaves A

The Falling Leaves B

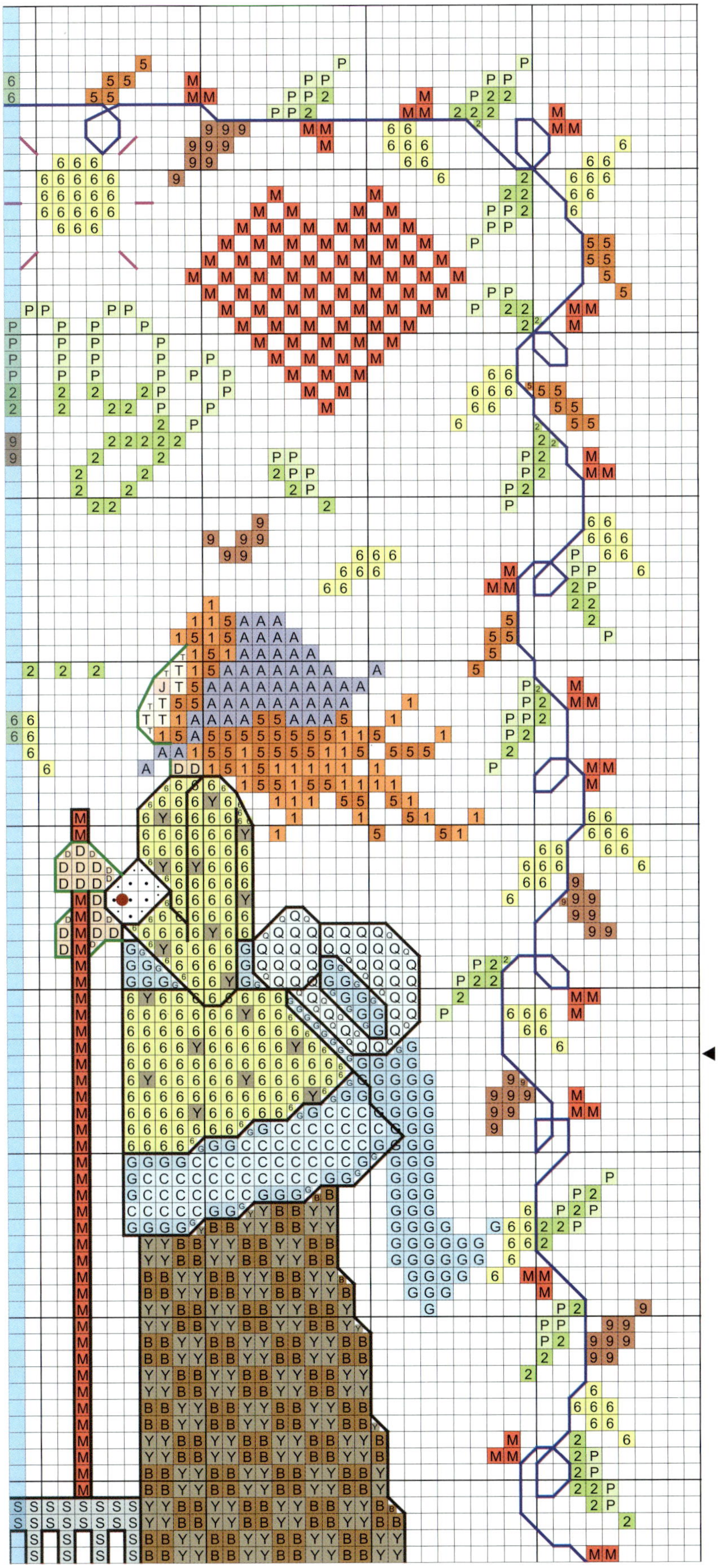

The Falling Leaves
Stitch Count = 106w × 124h

FABRIC SIZE

- One 15" × 17" (38.1cm × 43.2cm) piece of 14-ct. white aida

DESIGN SIZE

- 11-ct. = 9⁵⁄₈" × 11¹⁄₄" (24.5cm × 28.6cm)
- 14-ct. = 7¹⁄₂" × 8⁷⁄₈" (19.1cm × 22.5cm)
- 16-ct. = 6⁵⁄₈" × 7³⁄₄" (16.8cm × 19.7cm)

CROSS STITCH

ANCHOR		DMC	COLOR
002	•	White	White
1006	L	304	Medium Christmas Red
400	S	317	Pewter Gray
9046	M	321	Christmas Red
1014	9	355	Dark Terra Cotta
351	B	400	Dark Mahogany
265	2	471	Very Light Avocado Green
253	P	472	Ultra Light Avocado Green
326	N	720	Dark Orange Spice
324	U	721	Medium Orange Spice
302	6	743	Medium Yellow
301	E	744	Pale Yellow
1012	D	754	Light Peach
1021	J	761	Light Salmon
1004	5	920	Medium Copper
1003	1	921	Copper
1033	G	932	Light Antique Blue
1011	T	948	Very Light Peach
382	Y	3371	Black Brown
035	O	3705	Dark Melon
1032	C	3752	Very Light Antique Blue
1031	Q	3753	Ultra Very Light Antique Blue
122	A	3807	Cornflower Blue

FRENCH KNOT

ANCHOR		DMC	COLOR
9046	•	321	Christmas Red

BACKSTITCH

ANCHOR		DMC	COLOR
301	—	744	Pale Yellow
261	—	3053	Green Gray
382	—	3371	Black Brown
373	—	3828	Hazelnut Brown

Bright blue area indicates last row of previous section of design.

The Falling Leaves C

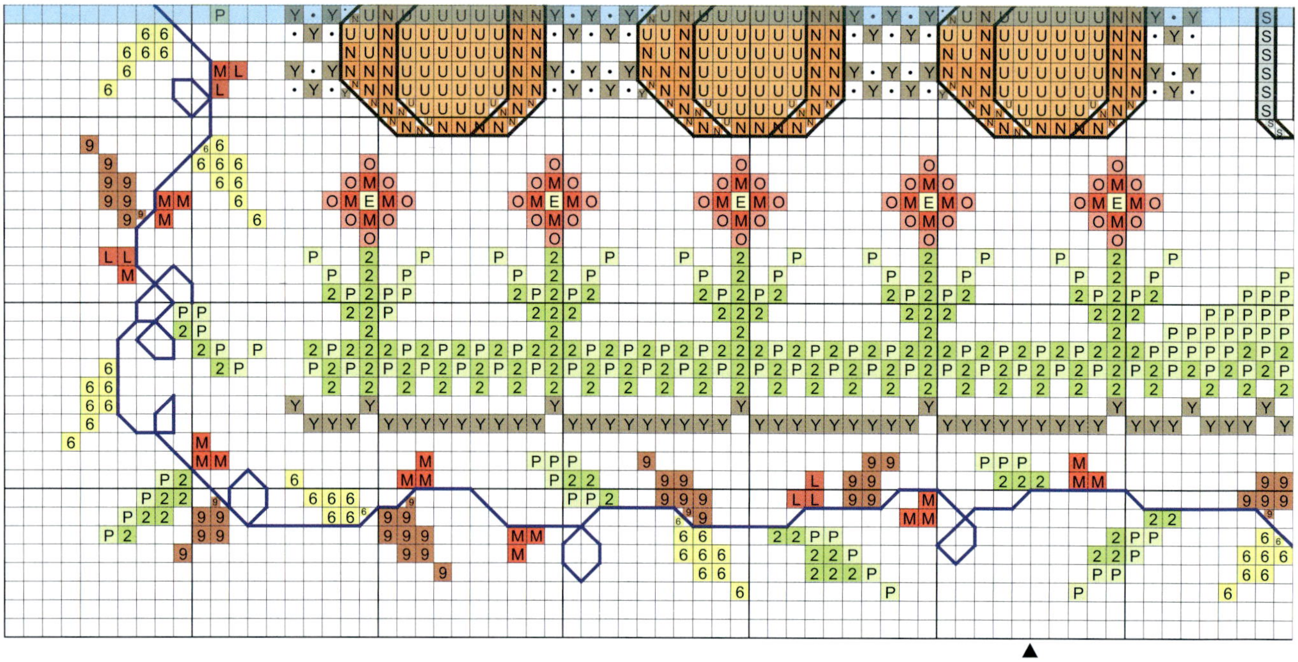

The Falling Leaves D

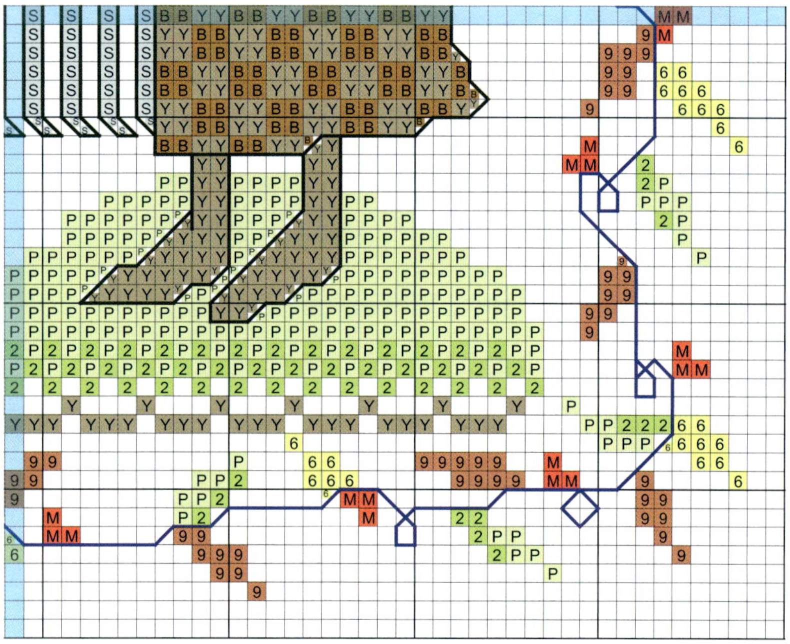

The Falling Leaves Chart Diagram

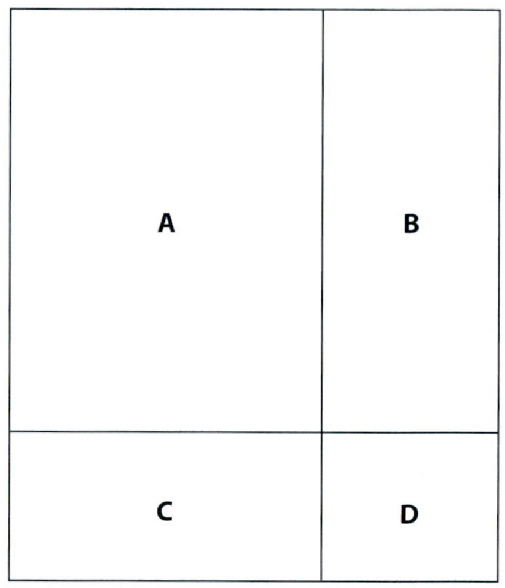

CROSS STITCH

ANCHOR		DMC	COLOR
002	•	White	White
1006	L	304	Medium Christmas Red
400	S	317	Pewter Gray
9046	M	321	Christmas Red
1014	9	355	Dark Terra Cotta
351	B	400	Dark Mahogany
265	2	471	Very Light Avocado Green
253	P	472	Ultra Light Avocado Green
326	N	720	Dark Orange Spice
324	U	721	Medium Orange Spice

CROSS STITCH

ANCHOR		DMC	COLOR
302	6	743	Medium Yellow
301	E	744	Pale Yellow
1012	D	754	Light Peach
1021	J	761	Light Salmon
1004	5	920	Medium Copper
1003	1	921	Copper
1033	G	932	Light Antique Blue
1011	T	948	Very Light Peach
382	Y	3371	Black Brown
035	O	3705	Dark Melon
1032	C	3752	Very Light Antique Blue
1031	Q	3753	Ultra Very Light Antique Blue

CROSS STITCH

ANCHOR		DMC	COLOR
122	A	3807	Cornflower Blue

FRENCH KNOT

ANCHOR		DMC	COLOR
9046	•	321	Christmas Red

BACKSTITCH

ANCHOR		DMC	COLOR
301	—	744	Pale Yellow
261	—	3053	Green Gray
382	—	3371	Black Brown
373	—	3828	Hazelnut Brown

Bright blue area indicates last row of previous section of design.

The Snowcapped Trees
Stitch Count = 100w × 123h

FABRIC SIZE

- One 15" × 17" (38.1cm × 43.2cm) piece of 14-ct. white aida

DESIGN SIZE

- 11-ct. = 9 1/8" × 11 1/8" (23.2cm × 28.3cm)
- 14-ct. = 7 1/8" × 8 3/4" (18.1cm × 22.2cm)
- 16-ct. = 6 1/4" × 7 5/8" (15.9cm × 19.4cm)

CROSS STITCH

ANCHOR		DMC	COLOR
002	•	White	White
1006	N	304	Medium Christmas Red
9046	O	321	Christmas Red
351	R	400	Dark Mahogany
265	T	471	Very Light Avocado Green
253	S	472	Ultra Light Avocado Green
324	U	721	Medium Orange Spice
302	H	743	Medium Yellow
301	I	744	Pale Yellow
1012	K	754	Light Peach
1021	L	761	Light Salmon
176	V	793	Medium Cornflower Blue
175	W	794	Light Cornflower Blue
1011	J	948	Very Light Peach
382	D	3371	Black Brown
035	P	3705	Dark Melon
1031	G	3753	Ultra Very Light Antique Blue
1037	Z	3756	Ultra Very Light Baby Blue
122	E	3807	Cornflower Blue

FRENCH KNOT

ANCHOR		DMC	COLOR
382	•	3371	Black Brown

BACKSTITCH

ANCHOR		DMC	COLOR
400	—	317	Pewter Gray
9046	—	321	Christmas Red
262	—	3052	Medium Green Gray
382	—	3371	Black Brown
122	—	3807	Cornflower Blue
373	—	3828	Hazelnut Brown

The Snowcapped Trees A

The Snowcapped Trees B